The First Word Series

'The First Word' series of books provides an introduction to the Orthodox Church, to her traditions, and to her thought, cast in a series of short, succinct, easy-to-understand, attractive, pocket-sized books that can be easily purchased at the back of parish churches and in bookshops, and read over a coffee or on a commute.

The name of the series alludes, of course, to the Word-made-Flesh, but also indicates that what the series sets out is not to be understood as the only word on any single matter. Indeed, anyone approaching the Orthodox Church by means of these texts would be encouraged, as they grow in their faith, to take their reading further and to deepen their understanding of the matters covered therein.

The First Word
on the
Orthodox Church

Father Jacob Siemens

ST SERGIUS PRESS

Published by St Sergius Press
12 Regina Terrace
Cardiff CF5 1GJ
stsergiuspress@gmail.com

British Library Cataloguing in Publication Data

The First Word on the Orthodox Church
Siemens, Father Jacob

ISBN 978-1-916514-02-7

The Rev. Dr James Siemens (Father Jacob) is a priest of the Archdiocese of Orthodox Churches of Russian Tradition in Western Europe, an active academic, and Orthodox Christian Chaplain at Cardiff University. He is also the rector of St Theodore and St Teilo Orthodox Church in Cardiff, Wales, a city he has, together with his wife and eight children, called home since 2005. Before this, he lived and served in Manchester, England, Saskatchewan, Canada, and St Kitts in the West Indies. He studied at the University of Manitoba in Winnipeg, Canada, McGill University in Montreal, and finally the University of Wales, Lampeter, where he undertook his doctorate and, later, a post-doctorate, both in patristics. His is the author of a monograph on Theodore of Tarsus, together with various journal papers, book chapters, and encyclopaedia entries, as well as the co-editor of a major new volume on Eastern Christian philosophy. He was elected as a fellow of the Royal Historical Society in 2012.

The First Word on the Orthodox Church

Contents

Forward to the *First Word* Series

This book may be your first introduction to the Orthodox Church and her traditions, or you may be a practicing Orthodox Christian wanting to deepen your understanding of things you experience all the time but take for granted. Regardless of your reasons for picking it up, though, it is important to keep in mind that there is much to know and experience beyond the basics contained in these pages.

Indeed, it is the intention of every book in this series to set out what the Orthodox Church believes to be true both about itself and the world; it does so, however, conscious of the fact that immersion in Christian life and understanding is a *process*. In other words, as we encounter aspects of the Orthodox Faith, we come to see their fullness only *gradually*. Whether we are talking about the Bible and how it is used by the Church, or the idea of the Holy Trinity, or what we think of the person and work of Christ, there is always going to be much more to learn than whatever we might be able to say in a small book, even if what we say in that book provides a sound starting point from which to explore further.

That is the motivation behind the *First Word* series. This small book currently in your hands represents the first few faithful lines in what can be a long, exciting, and fruitful conversation. Equally, it could be a simple but inspiring one-off introduction to a topic about which you may wish to know more, but about which you may need or want no further discussion. Either way, this first word on the matter can be trusted in its own right, and expanded upon if desired. Consider it this way: there can hardly be a person on the planet who has not grown up conscious of the automobile. Indeed, a toddler may point at their favourite car – even if only based on its colour – long before he or she understands its capacity to carry passengers and goods over short and long distances. Between that innocent age and young adulthood, however, the child's awareness grows to include a car's importance to the family, its prominent place on the neighbourhood streets, and even, perhaps, the fact that some of their friends talk admiringly about certain makes and models. Then come the driving lessons, and a complete change in perspective. Now cars have power: power to go fast or slow, power to grant freedom, power to do harm. Over time, though, the newly-licensed driver becomes a mature and experienced driver, and maybe they even do a little bit of mechanical tinkering – all of which gives them an even more extensive understanding. From our first recognition of cars, then, to our first time behind the wheel, to our first visit to the garage, there is a continuum of understanding. It is precisely a continuum, though; nothing of our earlier perception is negated by what comes later. From our first encounter with the Orthodox Christian Faith (by means of this series), to our later, more developed understanding, what we learn is on a continuum, and nothing that may come later should deny the things we encountered when we first got going.

Why is this so important to remember? Because the Orthodox Christian story is at once simple, beautiful, and approachable, as well as complex, intellectual, and profound, and any temptation we may have to limit it to one end of the spectrum or the other must be avoided.

What, then, might we expect from this series?

Our hope is that your most basic questions will be answered in a way that is entirely sound and consistent with the Orthodox theological and spiritual tradition, yet also entirely approachable and understandable. If a complete newcomer can read one of these books and go away with a greater sense for what the Orthodox Christian Faith is about, while an experienced Christian with a more developed theological vocabulary can likewise nod at what is written and discover something that is at least helpfully stated, then it will have done its job. It is entirely possible to be simultaneously accessible and sound, especially when both the writer and the reader are clear about the limits of the material being presented.

An important thing to remember, though, is that each volume in the series is limited in scope. If one title represents a first word on the Church, it is just that; if another title is about icons, it too, is just about that. While one book may be about the Church, however, and another about icons, the over-arching context is vital. Neither the Church nor icons, nor anything else with respect to the Orthodox Christian Faith is about anything outside of its fundamental understanding of God the Holy Trinity, the Person of Jesus Christ as fully God and fully Man, and the vocation He has set before us to be proclaimers of the Good News whilst becoming as He is.

May your exploration of Orthodoxy be fruitful, and lead you ever nearer the Truth. For this, after all, should be the pursuit of each and every one of us, faith or no faith, elder or newcomer, scholar or amateur.

Introduction

Walking into a church for the first time can be a daunting experience. If it is not something you are used to, the atmosphere can be intimidating. Only a visit to an historic cathedral or open country church may feel less so, as, in a place like that, it is possible to be just one more tourist, or just another passer-by taking temporary shelter from a sudden rain. But this experience of unease in a church need not be limited to the non-Christian; indeed, it is just as likely that a Christian of another tradition feels that way in an unfamiliar place of worship. And to almost anyone who has grown up in the West – be

1

that Western Europe, the Americas, or Oceania – Christian or not – an Orthodox Church will almost certainly represent something unfamiliar.

Yet for all the Orthodox Church may be a largely unfamiliar presence in the West, it actually has a long history of extending beyond the borders of its original home in Eastern Europe and the Eastern Mediterranean world.

So, for example, Russian missionaries had a presence in Alaska in the eighteenth century, while Europeans from many of the continent's Eastern countries – particularly Ukrainians – made their way to settle in Canada's West from the late nineteenth century. Greeks, meanwhile, began to enter the United States in large numbers at the beginning of the twentieth century, followed by a second wave of immigration only a few decades later. And, of course, Russian connections with France include both the royal patronage of Nice in the mid-nineteenth century as well as the significant Parisian diaspora that arrived in the wake of the Bolshevik Revolution of the early twentieth century. Importantly, all of these examples of Eastern European migration entailed the building of churches and the practice of Orthodoxy.

A consequence of these shifting populations is that where we might not expect to find an Orthodox church, there very likely is one. We just need eyes to see. In fact, in the capital of ancient Wales, a land historically dominated first by Latin Catholic tradition, then its Anglican successor, and more latterly Methodism (what the Welsh simply call 'Chapel'), there is a large and very beautiful Greek Orthodox church dedicated to St Nicholas, originally established to serve the Greek sailing community in the late nineteenth century. It might be best described, however, as a 'hidden gem', insofar as it stands off a major road in the literal shadow of a beautiful and rather prominent Anglican church, out of view of any but the most eagle-eyed. Yet to go in is to encounter a marvel of colour, scent, and, if at the time of a Liturgy, sound and movement. Equally, in the less-visited, more rugged, Welsh-speaking north of the country, the town of Blaenau Ffestiniog boasts a long-standing Orthodox presence, with a bilingual priest who is, himself, immersed in the life of the community, while serving the liturgical life of the church from both a beautiful chapel attached to his house, as well as a significant Anglican church building well adapted for the purpose.

For all this, where does one even begin to unpick what is happening? How can anyone be expected to 'understand Orthodoxy' when – on their own – the initial sensations of walking into a church are enough to cause bewilderment? And when the ideas they represent – fundamental as those sensations are to Orthodox practice – are numerous enough to warrant hours of discussion? Well, hopefully, a book such as this is a good start.

Of course, this book is not alone in the field: from the late Timothy (Metropolitan Kallistos) Ware's well-known and magisterial *The Orthodox Church*, to Katherine Clark's offering in the *Simple Guides* series, also called *The Orthodox Church*, there are innumerable works to choose from. In fact, if you were so inclined, Paul Evdokimov's *Orthodoxy* can hardly be surpassed for its comprehensive and theologically-astute exposition of the Orthodox tradition. But each of these works presents something quite different to what this small book does. Evdokimov's is weighty and academic; Clark's is accessible, yet because it is a more systematic presentation of the faith, the reader still needs to go searching for answers through many pages to find answers to the more immediate questions he or she may have. Ware's book, finally, while it remains high on most people's list of recommended reading, compels you to contend with historic controversies and wrestle with theological ideas for which you may not yet be equipped, or in which you may have no interest (at least to begin with!). In addition to these excellent volumes, however, there have been numerous pocket guides to Orthodoxy published over time which the reader might uncover on the shelves of a second-hand bookseller or in the discard box of a local library. Many of these, too, have their value, but there is also a reason why they may not have endured: the information they set out may now be dated, their style of presentation may no longer be of the sort that appeals to an internet-saturated audience, or their print-runs were simply very small to begin with. Whatever the case, this book seeks to address all of these issues. It is succinct without being superficial, up-to-date while remaining perennial, and existentially sensitive while remaining doctrinally sound.

What this book tries to do is present the Orthodox Christian tradition in terms that are recognisable from experience. As people inhabiting a world made up of infinite choice, unlimited access to information, and perpetual material and mental distraction, the questions and thoughts that arise for us today will, in many respects, differ to those that arose for people even as few as twenty years ago. When it is possible, for example, to pull a phone out of your pocket and, with the swipe of a screen, gain access to any number of religious ideas, what makes Orthodoxy anything more than one religious narrative among many? When religious extremism is to blame for so much violence since the dawn of the twenty-first century, why should anyone trust the claims of one religious tradition or community over another? Indeed, in light of the objections of the scientific materialists, secular humanists, and the early twenty-first century's radical atheists, why should they trust any religious claims at all, or give them a moment's consideration?

Of course, these are only a few of the questions we might be asking as we approach Orthodoxy. If we were to illustrate a person's approach to a religious tradition today by drawing a series of concentric circles, the questions I have just listed would merely represent the outermost circle.

Because once the enquirer has got past those questions, he or she is immediately confronted by, at the very least: 1. a physical space and its symbols (the church building and things like icons); 2. specific vocabulary (the language of Scripture, theology, and worship); 3. rituals, and history (both general, as it relates to the Church as a whole, and local, as it relates to the specific community) that will at once seem foreign. It is these latter questions – those that prevail once an enquirer has passed beyond the outermost circle – that this book sets out to answer. Whoever you are, and however many times you have crossed the threshold between the street outside and the warm glow of the temple – be it never, the first, or the thousandth – it is hoped that what you find on these pages is of some use to you, and that you may find in Orthodox Christianity a congenial and comprehensible place without any diminishment of awe and wonder.

1.

The Origins of the Orthodox Church

I want us to use our imaginations for a moment. In our minds, we're going to visit an Orthodox church[1].

---

[1] Orthodox Christians will sometimes, rightly, refer to their local church building, and to parts of its interior in terms carried forward from the ancient temple in Jerusalem. So, for example, the church may be called the 'Temple', and the altar area the 'Holy of Holies'. In this book, we will use the terms more common to Western ears, except when using the word 'Temple' makes it clearer that we are talking about the specific building in which Orthodox worship takes place.

Perhaps it will not be much of a stretch for you, as you have visited an Orthodox church building once before, so you simply need to recall what it was like. But it may be that you have never ventured into one, and so imagination, possibly informed by photos on the internet, is all you have to draw on. Either way, seeing as Orthodox Christianity is an inherently sensory religion, any introduction to it, shy of first-hand experience, must surely invite some sort of imaginative engagement.

Say, then, it is a chilly, overcast day. This should be easy for the British reader, but the precise location you imagine doesn't matter. More importantly, picture yourself on the pavement outside an Orthodox church. The door of the church is open, a warm glow seems to beckon, and you are intrigued. You wonder if you can look inside. You wonder what you will find.

The first thing you should know is that the answer to whether or not you can look inside is an unequivocal 'yes'. No matter who you are or what your background, you will always be welcome to look in, to walk in, even make a full inspection of what you find. No one will put pressure on you or expect you to join anything. The thing you may wish to know – or at least have a sense for – ahead of time, though, is what it is you will find; and this is where I need you to stay in character for a few more moments.

You have mounted the step from the pavement, and find yourself in the porch of the church. This porch is also known as the 'narthex' and used to be the place where penitents and catechumens – that is, those who were in need of reconciliation before returning to communion, and those who were in the midst of their training to become Christians – would stand for services, although it has been centuries since penitents and catechumens have been kept separate from other worshippers. Regardless, the narthex tends to be the place where, today, you might prepare yourself for worship before stepping into the 'nave' – that is, the main body of the church building. This preparation would be done simply by mentally and spiritually collecting yourself before going any farther into the building for a service. In that respect, the narthex is a place of transition: a place where you leave the street behind, and make yourself ready for the change in perspective you will experience when you take your next physical step.

You may have to pass through a door, or you may only pass over a line on the floor, but take a step further into the church and you are standing in the nave. The nave takes its name from the Latin word *navis*, which means 'ship', and is said to reflect the fact that the Church is the 'ark of believers' – that is, the ship of faith that carries us to safety over the course of life. The first thing that hits you now is the way it smells: indeed, incense may still hang in the air from the last liturgy (church service) that was served. In any case, incense is one of the first noticeable features of Orthodox worship, and one that can linger long after the last words of the liturgy have been sung. The smell of the church is certainly one of the first things newcomers comment on at their first visit, and may be one of the more beautiful, if non-customary, experiences of regular worshippers and one-time visitors alike.

The next thing that tends to strike people, and that you will notice at almost the same time as the smell of the church, is the fact that you cannot see the altar (holy table). People in the West, if they have visited almost any sort of church – especially be it Roman Catholic, Anglican, or Lutheran – will be accustomed to being able to see all the way to the front, where the altar, lectern, and pulpit are generally in plain view[2]. Not so in an Orthodox church. Instead, you will see a wall (or screen, or divider) at the East end of the nave that is covered in icons: a large image of Christ the Pantocrator (a word meaning, 'almighty' or 'ruler of all'), another large image of the Holy Virgin (whom Orthodox tend to call the 'Theotokos' or 'God-bearer'), possibly another large image of Saint Nicholas or the patron saint of the parish, and another of Saint John the Baptist (whom the Orthodox tend to call 'the Forerunner'). Between each of these substantial icons may be doors which are themselves adorned with icons: the 'Holy Doors' in the middle of the iconostasis, which will likely depict the

---

[2] In some Western churches – Anglican churches in particular – you may still find a 'screen' in place that divides the nave from the part of the church called the 'chancel' and 'sanctuary'. Indeed, in some of the earlier medieval churches that still stand in the British countryside, this screen may well be a solid stone wall. Because it is not the place of this book to explore the finer points of Western Church architecture, however, we won't get into detail here as to the distinction between one of these screens (or walls) and an iconostasis in an Eastern church. Suffice it to say that their appearance and significance is similar to, but not the same as, the iconostasis.

Annunciation and the four Evangelists (Saints Matthew, Mark, Luke, and John), then two single doors – one on each side of the iconostasis – depicting, perhaps, St Michael the Archangel on the left and St Gabriel the Archangel or one of the early deacons on the right. In a smaller row above this wall of large icons and the doors, is a series of icons depicting the principal events in the life of the Saviour. There could be even more rows, but in the first instance, your attention will be on the fact that this wall of icons, and the fact that the walls of the church all around you seem to be covered with them, is unlike every other experience you have had in churches before.

So now you stand in the middle of the church, with the smell of incense in the air and images of Christ, the Theotokos, and the saints around you. Perhaps there are candles lit in the votive stands near the iconostasis; perhaps you light one yourself. Regardless, your mind is rightly full of questions: What actually goes on in here? Whence did it emerge? What does it all mean? Because we will explore answers to the first and last of these questions over the course of this book (indeed, it is the purpose of this whole series!), the first thing we will look at here is the answer to the second.

Where did all the things you see when you first enter an Orthodox Church come from? What sort of culture gave rise to it? Simply put, the Orthodox Church, and much of what you see when you are inside one, emerged from Jerusalem with the first followers of Jesus Christ, in the first century A.D.. This does not mean that, after the ascension of Jesus, the Holy Spirit descended on the disciples and immediately there sprang forth a fully-formed community of Christians with exactly the same sorts of services and other practices – or even terminology for expressing the faith – as you will encounter today. Rather, the disciples of Jesus were Jews. They continued to practice the traditions of their faith, even as they sought to understand among themselves what the implications were of their experience with this remarkable teacher who died, rose again, and ascended into heaven. In conjunction with the psalms they sang and the words they listened to in the synagogues, though, they also met together to recount the stories of Jesus and, after reflecting on what they had learnt from him, broke bread together. In fact, this early picture of the Church is sometimes called 'Jewish-Christian', insofar as it is not yet clear that the early Christians aren't simply Jews with some additional beliefs and practices.

This begins to change, however, with the ministry of St Paul. The appropriately named 'Apostle to the Gentiles' draws on a profound understanding of his own Jewish faith and a sound training in the tools of Greek philosophy, and applies them both to his reflections on Jesus Christ. By doing so, he lays the groundwork for everything we would come to understand as a Church about the God-Man, establishing a sort of synthesis for thinking about God and what God accomplishes in Christ, that would serve all the early saints of the Church very well over the coming centuries. Both geographically and intellectually, St Paul leads the Church out of the synagogue and establishes it as part of the wider Roman world. In the process, though, the Church carries with it from the synagogue its hymn book (that is, the book of Psalms), as well as its attention to the words of the Law and the Prophets (what, bound together, we come to call the 'Old Testament') read in the context of the gathered assembly. Indeed, the practices of the synagogue become the 'Liturgy of the Catechumens'[3] in the Orthodox Christian worship of today. But importantly, the Church also carries with it a memory of the Temple in Jerusalem. Whereas the synagogue was centred on the Scriptures, the Temple was about sacrifice, with all of its corresponding rituals, vestments, and architecture. And these, interpreted in light of the Last Supper and Crucifixion, can be read as the basis for the 'Liturgy of the Faithful' in the Orthodox services.

So the Orthodox Church finds its origin in Judaism: something that can still be discerned in its liturgical practices today. But then the Church spreads, and while its practices remain connected to its Jewish memory, it starts to think like the Greek philosophers. This, in turn, gives it its distinctive theological tradition. Indeed, those men (and they were, for the most part, men) to whom we look for

---

[3] The Liturgy of the Catechumens and the Liturgy of the Faithful together make up the two 'halves' of the Church's Divine Liturgy: the service that Western Christians might call the 'Mass', the service of 'Holy Communion', or the service of the 'Holy Eucharist'. The two parts correspond, respectively, with the service (or liturgy) of the word and the service (or liturgy) of the altar in Western Catholic terms.

guidance as we do our thinking about God today and whom we call the Fathers of the Church, took what they knew about Christ from the Scriptures and from the oral traditions that were being shared wherever early Christians gathered. Then, processing it all through the lens of classical learning, they established what we might describe as the right ways – as well as the wrong ways – to understand who Christ was and what he accomplished when he walked among us as a human being. The right ways of thinking about Him we call 'orthodoxy' (from the Greek words 'orthos' – meaning 'right' or 'correct', and 'doxa' – meaning 'opinion' or 'praise'), while the wrong ways of thinking about him we call 'heresy' (from the Greek word 'hairesis' – meaning 'a choosing for oneself'). Orthodoxy as we know it, then, and as you encounter it in physical form when you first step inside an Orthodox church building, takes its initial shape in an ancient Jewish context, then moves out into the wider, Roman, world of the time, where its thinking is broadened and it develops more fully the ideas that become fundamental to Christianity as a whole. And it is this that you encounter when you

17

enter a church today, and behold all the symbols of faith that testify to Orthodox Christianity.

2.

The Development of the Church in the
First Three Centuries

It is almost impossible to describe Orthodoxy without starting with a bit of a history lesson, as so much of what you will find in Orthodox thought and practice today can be traced directly back to what happened in the first centuries of the Church's story. That's why it was important, in the first chapter of this book, to step into the church building and see the connections between what you first encounter there and the earliest days of Christianity in Jerusalem. But the picture would not be complete without also knowing what happened in the centuries between those early days and the legal recognition of Christianity in the early fourth century by the emperor Constantine. For this reason, we will spend at least a few moments exploring this story.

Upon looking around the church building in our first chapter, and seeing the icons on the iconostasis and the walls all around the building, it may be that you noticed the saints they depicted. Besides the Theotokos, this could typically include canonised theologians[4] such as Basil the Great,

---

[4] In the Orthodox Church, the word theologian is used in three ways. The first of these might be the most conventional, in the sense of referring to one who is formally educated in, and teaches, theology. The second is more pious, and is derived from fourth-century monk Evagrius Ponticus' declaration that a theologian is one who prays, and that one who prays is a theologian. Finally, there are three saints who bear the formal title of theologian: St John the Theologian, St Gregory the Theologian, and St Symeon the New Theologian. This formal status, however, does not preclude countless others from sharing in the theological project of the Church.

Gregory of Nyssa, Gregory of Nazianzus[5], and John Chrysostom, as well as beloved saints around whom are great stories such as Nicholas of Myra and Demetrius of Thessaloniki. Importantly, those depicted in icons may be men or women, theologians, martyrs, monastics, or missionaries. In fact, one saint I have personally included as an icon for veneration in my own parish is Irenaeus of Lyons. This is because, alongside the others, I see Irenaeus as one of those Church Fathers whose contribution to the development of Orthodox Christian thought is so substantial that we owe him a significant debt of gratitude. But regardless of whose images you find on the walls or on the stands around the church, they will almost certainly

---

[5] These three saints are, together, commonly called the 'Cappadocian Fathers', due to the fact that they were rough contemporaries who all came from the province of Cappadocia in what is now modern Turkey. Basil, who became bishop of Caesarea, was the older brother of Gregory, who would become the bishop of Nyssa. Gregory of Nazianzus, meanwhile, was their friend, and would eventually become Patriarch of Constantinople. All three made significant contributions to the Church's understanding of the doctrine of the Trinity, while showing that the Christian Faith could be taken seriously as an intellectual movement.

include the early Fathers who did so much to point us in the right direction when it comes to thinking theologically: about God the Holy Trinity; about Christ, in terms of who He is and what He did; about the Holy Spirit and His role in the Godhead and in the world; about the life of the Church; and about people, in terms of who we are and what we can look forward to in light of God's work for us. I want to look at the first three centuries of the Church in particular, though, not only because they were so instrumental in laying down the Church's intellectual foundations, but because there was so much else going on that caused the Church to grow and take shape.

The first thing that comes to mind in this regard is persecution. For prior to the legalisation of Christianity in A.D. 313, Christians went through numerous periods of persecution under various emperors. These persecutions saw Christians devoured by lions, run through with blades, crucified, and in at least one instance, used as human torches in an emperor's garden. Far from scaring off potential converts, however, the martyrdoms suffered at the hands of the authorities only served to galvanise those already committed to the Faith. Those not already convinced of it, meanwhile, seemed to come around if not to conversion, then at least to Christianity as a force to be reckoned with. Indeed, as Tertullian, the late-second century Latin Father from Carthage said, 'the more we are mown down by you, the more we grow in number. The blood of Christians is the seed,' which is often paraphrased as, 'the blood of the martyrs is the seed of the Church'. Whatever the case, the martyrdom that resulted from the persecution of Christians was instrumental in the growth of the Church.

Apart from persecution and martyrdom, another important feature of the development of the Church in the first three centuries is what we might call 'the discernment of Tradition.' This is of especial interest to Orthodox Christians, as 'tradition' is often the first port of call when it comes to establishing, explaining, or otherwise discussing points of faith. It might be said that, when confronted with a question about faith, the Orthodox first ask, 'What do the Fathers say?' then, 'What do the Scriptures say?', followed by, 'What does the Church say today?' There is a reason for this, though: a reason that can be easily located, for example, in the very argument that led to the first council of Nicaea in A.D. 325.

In this case, there was an priest in the Egyptian city of Alexandria called Arius, whose understanding of Christ was that he was created, and therefore not eternal – and certainly not of equal status with God the Father. Arius was opposed by the deacon Athanasius, who declared that Christ was by necessity equal to, and co-eternal with, God the Father. The historian Eusebius of Caesarea tells us how both men used the Scriptures, together with the 'words and traditions' of the Fathers, to sustain and bolster their arguments. From the Church's point of view, then, the fact that the ideas of Athanasius eventually won the day is a testament to the power of his arguments, his correct interpretation of tradition. In this process, meanwhile, the will of the Holy Spirit is discerned. Indeed, as the Christian Church was seeking to elucidate a sound theology, its contributors consistently did so with reference (and deference) to what had gone before. By this means, Tradition became the cornerstone of the Orthodox Christian edifice of thought.

Perhaps most importantly, though, the medium by which the tradition was communicated was the structure of apostolic ministry, which became the operative basis for the Church by at least the early second century. It begins with the bishops who, as direct successors of the apostles themselves, bear the responsibility of gathering the Christian community around them, handing on the traditions they had received (that is, the history and teachings of Jesus and his followers), and presiding at the Eucharist. Then, as part of this ministry – and as we read in chapter six of the Acts of the Apostles – deacons were ordained to maintain equitable distribution of the Church's resources among those in need. So deacons took on a more practical role. At the same time, while it is not clear at precisely what point presbyters (literally meaning 'elders', but rendered in English as 'priests'), an order of Church leaders also referred to in Acts (and elsewhere in the New Testament) became absolutely distinct from bishops, but they did indeed become distinct. Certainly by the early second century – so, within approximately eighty years of the Ascension of Jesus – they represented a ministry that was neither that of bishop nor deacon, but something closely related to bishop in function yet also delegated *by* the bishop like deacon. In other words, by the time St Ignatius of Antioch was writing his letters to various Churches in the first half of the second century, bishops were the leaders around whom the followers of Jesus gathered in the many centres of faith across the Roman Empire, and especially the Eastern half of the Roman Empire; priests shared in the work of the bishops, by taking on a delegated role in the communities outside of the city centres; and deacons assisted the bishop in making sure that the work of the Church in caring for its people was duly carried out.

In short, then, the Church at this early stage would best be described as 'primitive'. This means: 1) it remained very close to its liturgical origins in the Jewish synagogues and the memory of the Jerusalem Temple, 2) it was enduring persecution which at times could be extreme, and 3) its identity was becoming increasingly defined by *tradition* – which, in this case, meant the teaching and practices transmitted by the bishops, in concert with those they appointed to assist them in their task.

3.

Constantine and the Councils

The first historian of the Church, Eusebius of Caesarea – whose name we first encountered in the last chapter as the narrator of the conflict between St Athanasius and Arius, between Christian orthodoxy and heresy – tells us that in the year 312, the Christian Church took a significant turn. This was the year of the Battle of Milvian Bridge, the night before which the Roman Emperor, Constantine, had a vision. In this vision he saw either the sign of the Cross or the 'chi-rho' ('XP', which represents the first two letters of the title 'Christ', in Greek),[6] accompanied by the Latin phrase, *In hoc signo, vinces* (meaning, 'In this sign, conquer). Upon having this vision, he had his soldiers paint the symbol on their shields, after which they went forward and won the battle. Whatever the precise, historical, truth of this momentous event, though, the result was that not long after, Constantine first issued an edict of official tolerance for Christianity (called the 'Edict of Milan'), and not long after that, replaced traditional Roman practice with Christianity as the official religion of the empire.

We should not underestimate the significance of this moment. For even at this stage in history, Christian numbers around the Empire were hardly more than those of the followers of many other cults particular to the various regions of the Mediterranean world. For some reason, however, it was Christianity that gained imperial approval, and it was Christianity that would come to dominate the

---

[6] Eusebius reports that it was the Cross, while Lactantius, another early Church historian, reports that it was the 'chi-rho'. Whatever the case, it was a symbol that Constantine clearly understood as being representative of Christ and the Christian religion.

intellectual and religious life of the Empire forever thereafter.

Once Christianity was official, however, it was important to Constantine that it be unified for the sake of the Empire. In this respect, the rumblings of disagreement among Christians that had begun in Alexandria and spread around the Eastern Mediterranean, briefly mentioned in the last chapter, needed to be reined in. As we saw, Arius, an Alexandrian priest, had been preaching that Christ was created and, as such, was of a different nature to God the Father. Arius' argument was that if Christ shared His nature with God the Father, then God's essential oneness would be compromised. In support of his position, he drew on the scriptures and the tradition of the Church (as he understood it), concluding that, while Christ was clearly not a mere creature of the human sort – or even an angel – he had to have been created and, as such, was necessarily subordinate to the uncreated God. A deacon in the same city, Athanasius, thought otherwise. He therefore challenged Arius, and so began an argument that, if Eusebius is to be believed, spread beyond the threshold of the Church to the average person on the street. If he was going to have a united faith for a united empire, then, Constantine had his work cut out for him. His approach was to call the bishops of the whole Church together for a council, which he set in the city of Nicaea in the year 325.

This council would become the first in a series, setting a pattern for the resolution of theological disputes in the Church. Called together by the Emperor, attended by bishops representing the whole Church, and held in various cities of the Empire, there were seven such councils held between 325 and 787. These councils took the title 'ecumenical' (meaning that the decisions taken at these councils applied to the whole Church, across time and place), and served to establish what the Church understood about the relationship between the Persons of the Trinity, the nature of the Holy Spirit, and, perhaps above all, the doctrine of Christ.[7]

---

[7] The Ecumenical Councils were: **1) Nicaea I in 325** at which Arianism was condemned, and the first text of what we call today the 'Nicene Creed' approved, in which Jesus Christ is described as being 'of one substance with the Father'; **2) Constantinople I in 381** at which Apollinarianism was condemned (the idea that Christ had neither human mind or human soul), and the final text of the Nicene Creed approved;

In light of this, it might be said that the legalisation of the Christian Church under Constantine, followed by Christianity becoming the official religion of the Empire, enabled the explicit fusion of Scripture, Tradition, and reason, in an authorised and universally-accepted form of theological decision-making that would become the 'conciliar way'. Today's Orthodox Church bears the blessed responsibility of carrying on the life and teaching of the historic Church that first met in these councils, as the faith it follows and proclaims is the same as that manifest in the declarations and canons of the

---

3) **Ephesus in 431** which, in opposition to Nestorius, who implied by his language that Christ was merely man, established the title 'Theotokos' (God-bearer) for Mary as an affirmation that the child she bore was indeed truly God; **4) Chalcedon in 451**, at which the Church declared that Christ was fully God and fully man, joined in 'hypostatic union', in opposition to the idea of Eutyches, who posited that there was only a single, divine, nature in Christ; **5) Constantinople II in 553** at which certain Nestorian ideas were once again visited and condemned; **6) Constantinople III in 680**, which affirmed the fullness of Christ's two natures by repudiating the idea of *monotheletism*, which declared that Christ had only a divine will; **7) Nicaea II in 787**, which dealt with question of icons by declaring images of Christ and the saints to be of the true faith, and restoring their veneration.

seven Ecumenical Councils. Among other things, this is an important dimension of the confident assertion Orthodoxy makes that it has not changed or broken continuity with the faith and practices of the early Church.

4.

Fundamental Doctrines

It might seem strange that we should explore the fundamental doctrines of the Orthodox Church so many pages into a book like this, but we do so precisely because the history of the Church was such that its basic doctrines were not fully articulated until they had passed through the Councils. To be sure, the Church knew what it believed and Who it worshipped, but the precise formulae of words for that belief took some time to refine.

Even non-Christians today may have a sense for the fact that Christians believe in one God in Three Persons, and in the fact that the Son of God became man in Jesus Christ. But every one of those terms has far greater import than a mere cursory statement can express. In fact, that God is Trinity and that the Second Person of the Trinity took on flesh and became man is of such importance to Orthodox Christians, that almost every action we undertake in the Liturgy is done three times, that almost every word of prayer explicitly evokes the Three Persons, that we cannot read the Bible without doing so Christologically (i.e. through the interpretive lens of the Incarnation), and that even our personal gestures are done in a way that expresses both Trinity and Incarnation. Indeed, when we cross ourselves in the Orthodox Church, we do so with our index and middle fingers touching our thumb (signifying three-in-one), while our ring and little finger are kept pressed to our palm (signifying the two natures of Christ). In this sense, a 'mere' devotional act becomes a creedal statement.

And therein lie the two most essential doctrines of Orthodox Faith. Of course there is more, as the Creed composed by the Church over the first two

Councils both implies and makes plain. God being Three Persons means that each Person must be reflected upon equally, and in this respect, the Holy Spirit is both spoken about in the third paragraph of the Creed, and plays a fundamental role in the Divine Liturgy by means (at least) of His place in the Anaphora (the Eucharistic Prayer – the prayer offered over the bread and wine through which the elements are mystically transformed into the Body and Blood of Christ). After that, there is the doctrine of the Church: described as 'one, catholic, and apostolic'; there is the doctrine of baptism and the 'remission of sins'; there is the resurrection of the dead and the 'last things' (eschatology).

To treat each of these doctrines here is not our purpose. As interesting a prospect as it is (and it really is!), that would be the task of a different book. It is enough to say here that the Orthodox Church puts its faith in One God who is Three Persons: Father, Son, and Holy Spirit. This means that the Church understands God to be truly *personal*, but also *communion*. It is because of this communion that we can proclaim so confidently that God is love. Then, of course, there is no Orthodox Church without the Incarnation: the real, historical act of the

Second Person of God (the Eternal Word, the Son) taking on human nature and becoming a man, with all that this entailed. There are many dimensions to this basic proclamation, as well as further implications, that the Church took centuries to articulate, but all of these find their apogee in the Resurrection. Indeed, the Resurrection of Jesus Christ from the dead gives meaning to everything else He did whilst among us, and signifies the conquering of humanity's greatest fear and greatest problem. It determines how the Church understands the end times, and the very purpose of human life. The Resurrection grants immortality to humanity, and represents supremely God's loving nature.

The doctrine of the Church, then, is really just an extension of the doctrine of Christ. The Church is not so much a created thing as it follows naturally from Christ's work. Just as Jesus went about teaching and healing and manifesting the good news of God's eternal, redeeming love, so must the Church. It does this through word and action – and most especially in the administration of the Sacraments: mysteries instituted by Christ that deploy physical things to convey heavenly realities.

This is all made possible by the presence of the Holy Spirit in the Church – that is, the Third Person of the Trinity, who proceeds from God the Father, and enlivens the Church with God's real and abiding presence.

All of this makes possible the ultimate end of humanity, which is deification: our becoming like God. St Irenaeus, the great apologist of the late second century, first said in the preface to the fifth book of his *Against the Heresies*, that 'God became man in order that man might become God'. This very phrase was taken up by St Athanasius in his early fourth century work *On the Incarnation*, and has become a fundamental concept in Orthodox theology since. It denotes an exchange between God and humanity entailing, in the end, that humanity should participate in God's own nature, just as God participated in human nature. 2 Peter 1:4 puts it this way: '…by which have been given to us exceedingly great and precious promises, that through these you may be partakers of the divine nature…' (NKJV). Every doctrine of the Church, from our understanding of who God is to what He does to what He provides us, affects us by making possible our eternal salvation, which equates to nothing less than full participation in the Divine Life. Everything we have so far encountered in this book, and everything we will come to encounter, should be read with this, and all the other fundamental doctrines, in mind.

5.

The Fathers of the Church

In talking with an Orthodox Christian on almost any theological or spiritual topic, it will inevitably not be long before you hear mention of 'the Fathers'. And while there are other Christians who talk about the Fathers, such as Roman Catholics, Anglicans, and Lutherans, it is the Orthodox for whom these oft-unspecified figures represent so much more than mere historical characters.

The question is, then: who are these 'Fathers', and why are they so important?

Simply put, the Fathers are those theologians of the ancient Church who first articulated the Faith, both before and during the era of the ecumenical councils. The adjective we use to describe their work is 'patristic' (from the Greek word for 'father', *pater* or πατερ). In Orthodoxy, we do not necessarily stop using the word 'Father' at a given point in history, and while many of those to whom we refer as Church Fathers are named as saints, not every Father is one.

More concretely, the Fathers of the Church can be grouped into: 1) time period; 2) the locations in which they lived and worked; 3) the characteristics of their thought. So, for example, we first encounter what are called the 'Apostolic Fathers' – that is, those who worked in the period immediately following the deaths of the apostles, and are thought to have had direct contact with the apostles themselves. These include such figures as Saints Clement of Rome, Ignatius of Antioch, and Polycarp of Smyrna, and while the specific concerns with which they were most preoccupied varied in nature, they were at the forefront of establishing the template for Christian life and thought that we know today. After the Apostolic Fathers, we might consider some of those who emerged from a particular region and shared a common approach to philosophy that enabled the Church to more fully articulate its understanding of the Persons of the Godhead – that is, the Holy Trinity: the Father, the Son, and the Holy Spirit. In this case, there is a trio of theologians from Asia Minor who were especially important whom we call the 'Cappadocian Fathers', made up of Saints Basil the Great and his brother Gregory of Nyssa, together with their friend Gregory of Nazianzus. At the same time, when we divide the Fathers into 'Eastern' and 'Western', we do so on the basis that they are from one of two very broad regions – the Greek East or the Latin West. The Greek East includes the world extending from the Adriatic Sea between Italy and Greece to what today we call the 'Middle East', including Egypt. The Latin West, meanwhile, is easier to demarcate as all of North Africa west of Egypt, and all of Europe west of the Adriatic. And while these geographic divisions are crude, it is also broadly true to say that the Greek East expressed things differently to the Latin West, sometimes in complementary, sometimes in incongruous, ways. Some of the most significant Latin Fathers are Saints Augustine,

Ambrose, Jerome, Leo, and Gregory (the Great – who by the Orthodox is often called 'the Dialogist'). All of these latter figures are of immense importance for the nature of what they contributed to the Orthodox tradition and, in the case of Augustine at least, for the sheer extent of his writings. Indeed, St Augustine may be the most prolific theological author of any period, region, or school. But finally, there are also a few Fathers from beyond the frontiers of empire who express their thought in a different way to that of either their Greek or Latin compatriots, such as Saints Jacob of Nisibis, Ephrem the Syrian, and Isaac the Syrian. All of these come from the Syrian world, and if St Ephrem might be seen as representative of this group, his approach to theology is more poetic and less obviously interested in the philosophical methods and vocabulary deployed by either the Greeks or the Latins.

Being acquainted with the Fathers is a virtual condition of being Orthodox – not because every Orthodox Christian must have the same facility with historical theology, but because the Tradition of the Church is the single greatest touchstone in terms of determining what constitutes Orthodoxy. Indeed, without a central authority such as Roman Catholicism has in its pope, Orthodoxy must be in constant dialogue with tradition. At the same time, the culture of the contemporary Church – especially over the last century – has been such that the teaching of the Fathers has emerged as a force not dissimilar to legal precedent in the tradition of English Common Law. In other words, just as a lawyer or judge today might cite an historic case in determining the right course of action in a modern court room, an Orthodox Christian is almost duty-bound to draw on, and even cite, the thought of the Fathers – both general and specific – when navigating any theological problem, challenge, or question.

6.

The Place of the Bible

Having said that the Fathers of the Church are a veritable hallmark of Orthodox thought, it would be a grave mistake to conclude somehow that the Bible does not hold a pre-eminent place in Orthodoxy. In fact, the work of the Fathers of the Church, and every theologian since, has had to be predicated on the pre-eminence of Scripture or risk being rejected out of hand. This is a fact that precedes even the fixing of scriptural canon.[8]

---

[8] The word 'canon', in this sense, comes from the Greek 'kanon' meaning 'rule', and refers to the list of books officially accepted

This is a particularly interesting facet of Orthodoxy, as the Orthodox Church understands itself as having cultivated Scripture. What this means is that it was members of the apostolic community that wrote the Gospels. It was St Paul, an apostle, who wrote many of the letters (epistles). It was these people and their direct successors who determined what best fit into the canon of Scripture. In other words, it was the Church that wrote the contents of Scripture, and what the Church didn't write, it made the decision to accept from the Hebrew canon (which becomes the Old Testament). In light of this fact, who and what has preeminent authority – the Church or the Scriptures – is not really a question that pertains to the Orthodox. Scripture is indeed authoritative, but seeing as Scripture emerges from the life of the Church, how it is read and interpreted cannot really be separated from the Church.

---

by the Church as being authoritative. Importantly, the canon of Scripture is not something that was established all at once and in every place the same way; minor differences exist in the recognition, as well as the division and numbering, of books across the Christian tradition.

What, then, constitutes Scripture? Or perhaps more commonly, what is the Bible?

First of all, between the words 'Scripture', 'the Scriptures', and 'the Bible', there is no meaningful difference. 'Scripture' simply refers to 'writing', and 'Bible' refers to 'books'. Consequently, while one word may feel more appropriate than the other in a certain context or sentence, only one thing is denoted: the compilation of writings that both guide and reflect the Church's mind. This compilation, commonly called 'the Bible', it should now be clear, is not a book; it is, rather, many books all bound together under one cover. These books reflect many different genres of writing: some are mythological[9]; some historical, some instructive, some poetic, some prophetic. The Gospels, meanwhile, represent a

---

[9] The word 'mythological' is often used in a dismissive sense, as when we say a story is 'just a myth'. This is not at all the way the word is used in this context. With respect to the Bible, when speaking about myth or describing anything as mythological, we are talking about a story that tells of origins – of either a natural or a social phenomenon – featuring strong supernatural elements, and replete with meaning. Ideas of 'fiction' and 'non-fiction' have nothing to do with myth. A myth conveys deep meaning; it does not pretend to be an empirical report of a specific event.

genre entirely unto themselves, reporting on the life of Jesus Christ in a way that combines a theological and journalistic approach.

What we call the 'Old Testament' is what to the Jews is simply the Scriptures. In other words, the early Church simply continued to regard the writings inherited from their Jewish forebears as authentic testaments of God's revelation – a situation confirmed in the fourth century and so maintained by the Church across time. There is an interesting history behind precisely what books are regarded as forming part of the Old Testament, which accounts for the minor discrepancies between Christianity in the Latin West and Eastern Orthodoxy, but these discrepancies can be overemphasised. For in the Orthodox East, the text received was the Septuagint: the Greek translation of the Hebrew Scriptures that were best known from around the second century before the birth of Jesus unto at least His own time. Indeed, when Jesus quotes the Scriptures in the Gospels, He is always quoting the text of the Septuagint. It is this translation and compilation that the Orthodox still use today. By contrast, the Western Church has traditionally used the Vulgate: a fourth century

Latin translation by St Jerome, which drew on an older, previous series of texts called the *vetus Latina*, while using the Greek for reference in the process. This means that the East and West received an overall compilation of Old Testament texts that varied in a few instances, a fact reflected in how it is that books are listed, how chapters and verses are numbered and, on a few occasions, how long a specific book ends up being. Later, most Protestant movements would end up eschewing both the Septuagint and the Vulgate in favour of the Masoretic text, which is the same as that used in modern Judaism as the basis for the Jewish Scriptures. Notwithstanding Martin Luther's negative evaluation of the epistles of James and Hebrews in the New Testament, meanwhile, the twenty-seven books that form the New Testament canon have been shared across East and West by all Christian Churches and traditions from at least the fourth century.

The Old Testament can be divided into the first five books, which together are called the 'Torah'. These books represent what Jesus is referring to as the law when he speaks of 'the law and the prophets'. The five books, made up of Genesis,

Exodus, Leviticus, Numbers, and Deuteronomy, include most of the great stories of the Bible with which many people become familiar in childhood. Stories and figures such as the creation of the world; Adam and Eve; Cain and Abel; Noah and the Flood; Abraham, Isaac, and Jacob; Joseph, his brothers, and his expensive coat; Moses and the Egyptians; the Exodus and the Ten Commandments: these can all be found in the pages of the Torah. So too can much of the ritual and moral law that we encounter across the history of the Hebrew people, including the Jews of the time of Jesus, and even in the setting of contemporary Judaism in the Western world.

Alongside the Torah, we can find the Prophets such as Isaiah, Jeremiah, Amos, to name but three. There are, of course, many others, and the prophets are often divided into two groups – the major and minor prophets (these adjectives describing only the scope of what they contribute and not the quality!). With the prophets, there are also the historical books which tell, for example, about the entry of the Hebrews into the Promised Land, how the Hebrews first had a system of judges and how they eventually got a king, the dramas around the throne such as the conflict between Saul and David, and the reign of

Solomon. Finally, there are the Wisdom books, comprised of Psalms, Proverbs, Ecclesiastes, and Job. The Old Testament concludes, then, with an apocalyptic book, called 'Daniel', which asserts God's sovereignty over all peoples, as opposed to the idea that He was only one more local, or tribal, god.

The New Testament is a lot easier to understand. It begins with the four Gospels, Matthew, Mark, Luke, and John. The first three Gospels together are sometimes called 'synoptic', insofar as they share a common style and even certain passages. The fourth Gospel stands alone, insofar as it takes a more 'spiritual' approach to its account of how God became a man, and what He did while amongst us. These are followed by a single book of history, called 'The Acts of the Apostles' or, more usually, 'Acts'. After that, there are a series of epistles (letters), mostly written by St Paul, to the various church communities around the Eastern Mediterranean, the purpose of which was to instruct them in the doctrines of the Faith and how to live that Faith. Finally, there is a curious book appended to all of these called the 'Revelation of St John the Divine', or simply 'Revelation'. This book, like the

Book of Daniel, is an apocalypse, insofar as it represents a vision of the Apostle John of the end of time. The Church debated whether or not it belonged among the Scriptures at all before finally accepting it, but outside of the Church, it may well be one of the most misunderstood of all the books of the Bible. Despite first appearances, the book is actually one of hope, while serving as something of a prototype for the Church's Liturgy. Ultimately, the New Testament presents few of the problems of the Old Testament, insofar as the books generally have a single author, the genres they represent are both singular and immediately manifest, and the lens through which they should be read is clear: the God-man Jesus Christ.

7.

The Development of Form

While the Church has its beginning and its end in Christ, we experience the Church in this world as an organisation made up of people and, since the fourth century at least, buildings. Indeed, when it comes to 'church', the vast majority of us will think first of the stuff we see, and possibly very little – or even not at all – about the stuff we do not see. Despite this common perception, it is imperative to remember that the Church is actually a totality. In other words, the composition of its beliefs, its people (together with the structures of which they are a part), its activities (the things we do within it), and even its buildings, cannot really be separated out from one another. For all this, it is inevitable that, in order to understand the Church more thoroughly, we are forced to break it down into parts. Because we have learnt a little over the initial chapters of this book as to what the Church believes and how those beliefs developed, we will label that material the Church's 'content', set it aside for the time being, and move on to look at the Church's people and structures, which here we will call its 'form'.

Importantly, the development of the form really came about in a manner parallel to, and at roughly the same rate as, the content. So, for instance, as we see very clearly at the end of the Gospels of Matthew and Mark, something of the Church's form is conferred on Jesus' disciples. Immediately before His ascension into heaven, the Lord explicitly commissions His friends to go out into the world and baptise the nations, thereby revealing one of the primary activities of the Church: mission. And from that moment on, informed by the Holy Spirit who is fully manifest to these same friends when they are gathered in Jerusalem for Pentecost, their mission begins to grow.

Of course, there are other moments in the Gospels in which the seeds of the Church's external life are planted, including when Jesus declares to His disciples that they are given the power to forgive and retain sins, and when Jesus commands them to partake of the bread and wine 'in memory of me'. All of these we can assemble into a category called 'things that the Church does', including: baptising and chrismating (confirming) – that is, the actual making of Christians; reconciling people with God and with one another through the forgiveness of sins; feeding the faithful with the Lord's Body and Blood; uniting people in marriage; anointing them for healing; and ordaining others to carry on the same work. When the Church performs these things, they are called 'sacraments', and they are the foremost aspect of the Church's form.

We can, of course, also include preaching as one of the Gospel imperatives, even if preaching in its earliest form could not have consisted of expounding on the Scriptures. The texts of the New Testament, after all, are in many ways the *record* of early preaching and were not around in a form on which they could be expounded. This would not happen for another hundred years. While, for example, it is clear from his letters that St Paul the Apostle exhorted new Christians to live a life worthy of their calling, apostolic preaching largely meant telling the Good News of Jesus Christ by means of recounting the story of His life and work, and interpreting that story in a way that would stir up the listener into some form of response.

But what else makes up the visible life of the Church? In addition to the external work of the Church – that is, serving the sacraments and preaching – there is the fact that it is a community of people, all of whom have become part of the Body of Christ, all of whom have their own roles. There are bishops, priests, and deacons; but there are also subdeacons, readers, cantors, and acolytes (servers), and there have been other orders too, from time to time. There is the laity (from the Greek 'laos', or λαός, meaning 'people'), any of whom may have particular roles, but all of whom take up the primary role of follower and worshipper of Christ. And there are monastics: men and women, monks and nuns, who may live in community or, in the Western context especially, may live on their own, but whose lives are dedicated to living out the life of faith without the same compromises that have to be made by those Christians who live in the world – that is, lives that include the sorts of concerns everyone must face and that distract us from prayer, fasting, and worship. At least that is the ideal. In fact, many of the monastics living on their own in the West have to work very hard to make a living in much the same way as their married counterparts. We will say more about monasticism later.

Without the people, of course, there simply is no Church. The aspects of its form we have just described, though, arose when the disciples (who, now that they are 'sent' into the world are called 'apostles'[10]) travelled across the Mediterranean world and beyond, overseeing communities of followers and ordaining first deacons, then presbyters (whom we come to call 'priests' in English), to act together with them in service to these communities of followers. Deacons appear very

---

[10] The English word 'disciple' is derived from the Latin *discipulus*, and was used to translate the Greek word 'mathetes', or μαθητής, meaning pupil or follower. 'Apostle', by contrast, passes into English directly from the Greek 'apostolos', or ἀπόστολος, and means delegate or ambassador.

early indeed, as we read in the first six verses of chapter six of the *Acts of the Apostles*:

> *Now in those days, when the number of the disciples was multiplying, there arose a complaint against the Hebrews by the Hellenists, because their widows were neglected in the daily distribution. Then the twelve summoned the multitude of the disciples and said, "It is not desirable that we should leave the word of God and serve tables. Therefore, brethren, seek out from among you seven men of good reputation, full of the Holy Spirit and wisdom, whom we may appoint over this business; but we will give ourselves continually to prayer and to the ministry of the word." And the saying pleased the whole multitude. And they chose Stephen, a man full of faith and the Holy Spirit, and Philip, Prochorus, Nicanor, Timon, Parmenas, and Nicolas, a proselyte from Antioch, whom they set before the apostles; and when they had prayed, they laid hands on them.*

The nature of deacons and the service they are to render is fully embodied in this short passage, including the rationale for their order, their selection, and their ordination. The development of the priesthood, by contrast, is less clear: a consequence of the merging of different terms, derived from Christ's own ministry and embodied in the work of the Apostles, but devolved to auxiliaries as the numbers of followers of Jesus grew. So, for example, later in *Acts* we read a long discourse from the apostle Paul to the elders of the Church of Ephesus[11] in which they are referred to as presbyters (πρεσβυτέρους, acc. pl. of πρεσβύτερος in v. 17), and overseers (ἐπισκόπους, acc. pl. of ἐπίσκοπος, v. 28). These words, 'presbyter' and 'episcopos', denote a senior role that is not just chronological (*i.e.* based on age or longevity of service), but functional – that is, based on responsibility. It is clear, meanwhile, that when Paul uses these words, he is drawing them from the model of Christ the eternal High Priest – which means that, although the titles on their own do not necessarily imply a priestly character such as we

---

[11] Acts 20:17-36

understand the word 'priest' today, they must be understood in the context of the Priest from whom they derive. Finally, the fact that Paul, a chief apostle, should be addressing the elders of a Church thus, suggests an already-developing distinction between what we might call senior apostolic work, and some facet of that apostolic work undertaken vicariously.

Before the Apostles' deaths, meanwhile, they transmit their authority to successors. This authority entailed, meanwhile, the responsibility to maintain the Gospel, including its doctrine and the traditions around it that have been laid down in the decades following Pentecost. This transmission is called 'apostolic succession, and it leads us into the 'sub-apostolic' period: with the beginnings of a structured community made up of many, diverse smaller communities, all of which gather together to listen to the proclamation of the Scriptures, to sing hymns (the Psalms, together with verses of apostolic origin), and to share in the Eucharistic meal. These communities are led by the apostles' successors together with the priests and deacons who act together with them to maintain order, to ensure that the gatherings are properly convened, and to preside over the Eucharist.

We are now going to skip over a great deal of history, through the course of which all the things we have just noted become solidified and formalised. The numbers of communities grow and get organised into dioceses, the successors of the apostles become bishops in a way that we would recognise today, and their assistants – the priests and deacons – take on the formal role of serving the local Christian communities liturgically and pastorally. Consequently, the Church, by the time the Roman Emperor, Constantine, facilitates its emergence from the catacombs in the early fourth century, covers the length and breadth of the Mediterranean and beyond, by means of geographical regions inherited from the Roman Imperial administrative system, called 'dioceses', often named for their chief city. At the head of each diocese is a bishop, while under the bishop are smaller Eucharistic communities called 'parishes', that are more locally focused than dioceses. These parishes are served by priests (who stand in for the bishop), together with deacons (whose role, by now, is both liturgical and practical). In fact, this form of the Church becomes almost synonymous with Christianised Europe, especially by the end of the seventh century, by which point Islam had emerged from the Arabian Peninsula and separated the Christians of Asia and Africa from those to the north of the Mediterranean.

Between East and West throughout the first millennium, the Church would have been hardly distinguishable in form. Certainly, monastic life looked different on each side of the 'border'[12], bishops, priests, and deacons dressed slightly differently, theological language and methods diverged, and the Liturgy looked different; but the sense of attachment people felt to the Church as a reassuring power in the land, with its hierarchy and

---

[12] There was, of course, no hard border between what constituted 'East' and 'West'. Even after the Germanic tribes descended from the northern half of the European continent, putting pressure on and even penetrating the Roman Empire, the Eastern Churches remained in conversation with the West. It was Charlemagne's coronation as Holy Roman Emperor on Christmas Day, A.D. 800, that a turning point was reached, and from that point on it becomes possible to identify and observe the gradual disintegration of relations between East and West based on different ways of thinking. This growing disparity in content eventually led to a pronounced break in form.

the sense of connection across time that it proffered, was the same. Between the fourth and the eleventh centuries, through massive demographic change and corresponding political upheaval, the Church was a stable and stabilising force from Asia Minor to Ireland, and it might be argued that in the centuries since, people in East and West alike have been living with its legacy, especially in terms of social, political, and moral assumptions.

8.

The Church in Action

People's first point of contact with the Church now, as it has been since it began to outgrow the reach of individual apostles, must surely be the parish and its priest. This is because priests are the ministers of the Church most closely connected with where people are, due to the responsibility they have for presiding over the local Eucharistic community. Indeed, there is a high likelihood that a priest walking down any street in the world today will be recognised as such, and if spoken to by a member of the public, will be asked where his church is. People across the Western world, as well as Eastern Europe and much of the Middle East, have been steeped in a culture that has known the presence of priests for centuries and, religious or not, they retain a memory of this.

In Western Europe, it is likely the priest serves on his own, because after the sixteenth century, ordained roles in the Church became increasingly professionalised and opportunities for the less theologically-educated to serve in an ordained capacity correspondingly decreased. The result is that it is unlikely a local person, such as a committed farmer or tradesman, taught the services in order that he might serve as a deacon in the parish, would be able to do so. In Eastern Europe, however, where the idea of the seminary did not exert the same influence until later (and then to a lesser degree), even a small village parish might enjoy the services of a priest, a deacon, and possibly members of the minor orders. Nonetheless, any initial experience of the Church today is likely to consist of meeting a local priest (who may be married, or may also be a monk); attending services where there may, or may not, be a deacon present; being aware that this priest represents a bishop who resides in a different city; hearing about a monastic community somewhere that is admired by the faithful who have visited on retreat; and partaking in a social life that will likely include talk about favourite Orthodox books and (at least some) Greek, Slavic, or Middle Eastern foods.

One way of illustrating this is to consider a concrete example, and there is unlikely to be a better one than the Archdiocese of Churches of Russian Tradition in Western Europe, based in Paris, France (and which we will hereafter refer to as the 'Paris Archdiocese').

There are, in fact, three jurisdictional 'divisions' of the Russian Church in Western Europe as a result of the upheaval in Russian society from 1917 to 1923: the parishes that respond directly to the Moscow Patriarchate; the Russian Orthodox Church Outside of Russia (ROCOR), which saw itself as maintaining the specific mission of serving Russians in diaspora while rigorously upholding the traditions of the Russian Church, even when that meant being somewhat marginalised within the Orthodox world for a time; and the Paris Archdiocese, which held an important place in French and Russian intellectual circles in the first half of the twentieth century, and ended up extending its reach even across to North America due to the influence of the St Sergius Institute (l'Institut St Serge) on St Vladimir's Seminary in New York.

The Paris Archdiocese, meanwhile, exists today in most of the countries of Western Europe, from Germany in the East to Ireland in the West, from Italy in the South to Norway in the North. The greatest number of its parishes, however, is in France. The specific ethos of the Archdiocese is one of openness to the West – in the same way that the Word of God was open to the people among whom He took on flesh. That is, the Archdiocese believes its mission to be very much focused on being the Orthodox Church of the land in which it finds itself, of maintaining a respect for creative, yet entirely-faithful, theological enquiry, and of participation in the Church's life on the part of all its people – from bishops to lay parishioners.

If someone, therefore, were to visit a community of the Paris Archdiocese in Britain, then, they would likely encounter a priest serving on his own in a small parish. That parish would worship primarily in English, and in the course of worship, would commemorate the Patriarch of Moscow (seeing as the Paris Archdiocese is now an autonomous part of the Moscow Patriarchate), as well as its own Metropolitan Archbishop in Paris. Within the parish might be people from a number of ethnic backgrounds, but also converts from the Catholic, Anglican, or Protestant Churches, or even from no faith background at all. Because the priest will likely work in secular employment, there may be a reduced service schedule, but this may also be because the community does not worship in a building of its own. Indeed, such a parish will likely use a building they rent from another Christian community and have to work around their needs. In light of this, it is necessary for the Orthodox parishioners to be well-catechised in order that they are equipped to keep Orthodox practice even when there is no opportunity to experience a Feast Day, or some other special observance, locally.

This is not to say that every parish in the West looks like this. Across Canada and the United States, as well as Western Europe and Oceania, there are numerous Orthodox parishes in all of these regions that are well-established and able to offer a fuller liturgical schedule, and other celebrations and programmes that accord well with parish life. Local circumstances, together with the history of a specific jurisdiction will all have a bearing on whether or not a parish has its own building and a priest who can serve without taking secular employment. Whatever the case, Orthodox communities in the West today – perhaps because of their mixed circumstances, and especially when it comes to certain jurisdictions – often have a missionary outlook, and a strong sense of the importance of good theology and liturgy.

What of worship, though? We have heard, above, about the Divine Liturgy, but when we speak about parish life and the possible constraints on serving in the contemporary West, we should be clear about what it is we are actually speaking. And so we turn to our next section.

9.

The Form of the Church in its Services[13]

At the heart of Orthodox life is the Divine Liturgy. Indeed, where it has been said that 'to find out what a Christian believes, see how they

---

[13] There will be a number of vocabulary terms used in this chapter with which you will likely be unfamiliar. Do not feel you need to remember them all, and do not let them get in the way of the important ideas the chapter is seeking to convey. What matters most is that you finish the section with a greater understanding of what the Divine Liturgy is, and the part in plays in Orthodox Christian life.

worship', nowhere is this more true than in Orthodoxy. This is because the Divine Liturgy is the Church's response to Jesus Christ's command to 'do this in memory of me'. It is also the reason that this chapter comes with a warning: it is by a good measure the longest in this book. Indeed, the topic of the Liturgy could occupy a book of its own and still not be exhausted, so while this volume is dedicated to a first word on the Orthodox Church as a whole, the treatment given to the Liturgy here will be necessarily condensed; but it will still be longer than any other across these pages.

In the Divine Liturgy, the people gather, while on the Altar the common elements of bread and wine are transformed into the Body and Blood of Christ. The people then receive this sacred food, and so return to the world outside as literal bearers of God in their person.

Wonderfully, the title 'God-bearer' (or, in Greek, 'Theotokos') is a word used for Mary, the holy Mother of God, and so in this respect, we take on something of her character when we partake of the Eucharist, and especially when we fulfil our mission to carry Christ into the world. The Divine Liturgy is, in fact, replete with iconological implications such as these, and involves our transformation in all sorts of ways. Yet while we might distil the Divine Liturgy down to its most fundamental purpose, it entails a good deal more in terms of actions and movements than a priest standing on the Altar and offering a series of words over bread and wine.

The Liturgy is, in fact, something of a divine play. Like a play, it includes scripted words and movements meant to communicate something. Unlike a play, however, what is being communicated is a reality we do not normally perceive, and there is no 'audience' in the sense that there is a passive group of people present to receive the message. In the Liturgy, everyone present becomes an actor; everyone, from the people at the back to those serving on the Altar, become essential players in the divine action. The presence of the Lord is effected in the assembly by the mere utterance of an 'amen'.

At the same time, like a play, the Liturgy can be understood to unfold in 'acts' and 'scenes'. And to make it easier to understand, we will break it up into two acts with four scenes each.

The first 'act' is called the 'Liturgy of the Catechumens', and it takes up the first lot of time you spend within the service. The second 'act' is called the 'Liturgy of the Faithful', and it makes up the second, and last, half. There is a clear transition between these two, as the deacon (when present) actually leads the people in the 'Litany of the Catechumens', which concludes when he proclaims 'As many as are catechumens, depart; catechumens depart; as many as are catechumens depart. Let none of the catechumens remain'. This is immediately followed by a 'Litany of the Faithful', for which all of the faithful are then invited to remain and participate in the second act.[14]

---

[14] Catechumens are those who are preparing for entry into the Church (i.e. those who are preparing for baptism and chrismation). Traditionally, they would have been present only for the first part of Liturgy, during which time they would have heard the Apostol (a reading from the New Testament, especially one of the letters of St Paul), the Gospel and, most often, a sermon. By this means, their instruction in the Faith would have been grounded in liturgical practice and the hearing of Scripture. The Faithful, by contrast, are those who have been fully received into the Faith, and are ready to partake in the Mystery of the Altar.

Just as there are two acts, each can be divided into four parallel scenes. The first of these is *preparation*. In both instances, the preparation consists of hymns and litanies: a series of petitions on behalf of all the people for specific intentions, these led (where possible) by a deacon. After the preparation in each case comes an 'entrance' or *procession*. In the first case, it is the 'small entrance' during which the Gospel is borne by the deacon, together with the priest and servers, through the North Door of the iconostasis, and back through the Holy Doors in the middle. In Greek tradition, this will often entail walking through the midst of the people in the nave of the Temple before returning to the Holy Doors, while in the Slavic tradition, it is more likely to entail a shorter path from the North Door straight to the Holy Doors. Later, in the second instance, it is the Holy Gifts (the holy bread on the diskos, with the wine borne in the chalice) that are carried – this time by the priest and deacon together – until they again stand before the Holy Doors. After

---

Although the Catechumens are exhorted to depart from the Temple before the Church proceeds with celebrating this Mystery and this is still practiced in some places, they have not normally been expected to depart for many centuries.

73

this, both are *presented*: the Gospel by proclamation; the bread and wine by means of the Eucharistic Prayer (called the *Anaphora*). By each, these sacred things are manifest as something new. The Gospel is transformed from a static word on the page to a living thing in the hearts of the hearer; the bread and wine from common elements to the true Body and Blood of Christ that will become a living thing in our own bodies. The final scene, then, is what we might call *integration*. This is the moment whereby the Gospel is processed by means of the sermon, while the Body and Blood of Christ are physically consumed by those who are properly prepared for it. In summary, then, the Liturgy may be said to look like this:

- **Act 1 Scene 1**: **Preparation** (for our transformation by the Gospel)
- **Act 1 Scene 2**: **Procession** (of the Gospel)
- **Act 1 Scene 3**: **Presentation** (during which the Gospel is manifest as the Living Word)
- **Act 1 Scene 4**: **Integration** (during which the Mystery of the Gospel is taken on by the hearer by means of the sermon)

- **Act 2 Scene 1**: <u>**Preparation**</u> (for our transformation by the Body and Blood of Christ)
- **Act 2 Scene 2**: <u>**Procession**</u> (of the bread and wine)
- **Act 2 Scene 3**: <u>**Presentation**</u> (during which the gifts are manifest as the Body and Blood)
- **Act 2 Scene 4**: <u>**Integration**</u> (during which the Body and Blood are taken on by the communicant by means of eating and drinking)

But if it is that simple, some might wonder, why does the Orthodox Liturgy seem so elaborate and ritualistic? And they are right to wonder. A Liturgy sketched in 'acts' and 'scenes' is only a skeleton, whereas the Liturgy we experience is one of symbolic actions that include sound, sight, smell, touch, movement. The Liturgy we experience is a living mystery.

Although many prayers of preparation on the part of the priest have preceded it, the Divine Liturgy rightly begins with the chanted proclamation, 'Blessed is the Kingdom of the Father, and of the Son, and of the Holy Spirit', to which the people respond, 'Amen'. At this moment, the Temple is likely still filled with the smoke of incense from the time that the deacon[15] walked around and censed the Altar, the icons, and the people, cloaking all in the cloud of sanctity in preparation for worship. It is the moment of 'crossing the threshold', whereby those in attendance step from materiality into transcendence. Once that line is crossed, then, everything becomes an icon of heaven; every person in attendance becomes a witness to, and participant in, divine acts: they become united with the angels and saints in worship, the apostles in their ministry, and Christ in His Body.

The first of these acts is the Litany of Peace: a longer litany by which the principal petitions of the whole Church are brought forward, and which provide the setting for the rest of our worship. Following this, there is the first antiphon (very often a Psalm), then a short litany, the second antiphon and the Hymn to the Only-Begotten, another short

---

[15] Instructions for the Liturgy assume that a deacon is present to assist the priest. In parishes and at services where there is no deacon, the priest normally undertakes these functions together with his own. In the description of the Liturgy provided here, the presence of a deacon is assumed.

litany, and the third antiphon (normally, the Beatitudes). It is during this third antiphon that those on the Altar process with the Gospel, which itself is taken from the Holy Table and carried out of the Altar via the North Door, where it is then held aloft before the Holy Doors until the conclusion of the antiphon. Then, with the call of 'Wisdom! Stand aright!', it is walked through the Holy Doors, and replaced on the Holy Table.

While the choir sings the troparia[16] appropriate to the day, the priest says the 'Prayer of the Thrice-Holy', and when the troparia come to an end, he completes the prayer, and the people sing 'Amen'. This leads straight into the Trisagion[17], in which God

---

[16] The troparion and kontakion are separate, short, hymns with designated tones, that express the liturgical theme of the day – be it a Sunday, or the feast of a saint. The tones of those sung on a Sunday for the Divine Liturgy are divided into eight, and are called the 'Resurrectional Troparia'.

[17] The Trisagion may be replaced with one of two other hymns here: one beginning 'Before Thy Cross we bow in worship', and another beginning 'As many as have been baptised into Christ', the former being used particularly on the two days in the year when we commemorate the Cross on which Christ died; the latter being used, for example, on the Feast of the Nativity, the Theophany, and at Pascha.

is praised three-fold with the words, 'Holy God! Holy Mighty! Holy Immortal! Have mercy on us'. It is a solemn moment during which the priest proceeds to the East end of the Altar and blesses the 'Chair on High' which represents the throne of God, and is where the bishop – if he were present – would then sit. A priest would never sit in this chair, but rather turns and faces West, while standing just to the north of it, until the end of the Trisagion.

After the Trisagion, there is a dialogue between reader and priest, immediately following which the reader chants the prokeimenon and the apostol.[18] The Altar and people are then censed in preparation for the proclamation of the Gospel while singing the 'Alleluia', and the deacon emerges through the Holy Doors to chant the appointed passage for the day. As suggested in the above analogy with a play, the Gospel is really proclaimed in two phases, though.

---

[18] The prokeimenon is a series of verses in the tone of the Sunday or the feast, that often precede a reading from the Scriptures. In the case of the Divine Liturgy, the Scriptures then chanted are taken from one of the letters of St Paul, or some other book in the New Testament save the Gospels (which are proclaimed shortly thereafter), and the Book of Revelation (which is never read liturgically).

First and foremost is the moment in which it is chanted, then it is elaborated upon by the preacher. It is normal for the priest to stand before the ambon[19] and offer a sermon that 'translates' the meaning of the Gospel into words that connect it people's experience.

The Liturgy continues when the priest returns to the Holy Table and closes the Holy Doors and, while an 'augmented' litany[20] is led by the deacon, begins to prepare the Holy Table for the placement of the Holy Gifts which will soon be carried in at the Great Entrance. With this, the first part of the Liturgy, the Liturgy of the Catechumens, is swiftly coming to an end. After the Augmented Litany

---

[19] The ambon is a platform in the middle of the nave (the place in the Temple proper to the people), on which the bishop enthroned when he is being vested at the beginning of the Liturgy and remains until the Small Entrance with the Holy Gospel. Smaller centres do not necessarily have a formal ambon in the middle of the Temple, and instead use the base of the steps just outside of the iconostasis on which the deacon will stand as he leads the litanies.

[20] The Augmented Litany is a litany in which the people respond to each petition with a three-fold 'Lord, have mercy', and begins with the exhortation to pray with 'all our soul and with all our mind'.

comes the Litany of Catechumens, which concludes with the command for catechumens to depart from the assembly, and during which the preparation of the Holy Table concludes. As mentioned, although the tradition of catechumens leaving the Temple is still carried on in some parishes and monasteries, it is not common, and for the most part today catechumens remain and stand witness to the holy mystery that will unfold in the succeeding part of the Divine Liturgy.

By means of the dismissal of the catechumens from the assembly, then, we segue into the Liturgy of the Faithful in the form of the Litany of the Faithful. This is actually comprised of two short litanies, during which the priest offers two prayers in silence on the Altar before which the Holy Doors are opened, the whole Altar, the Iconostasis, the people are censed, and all the ministers of the Altar make their way to the Prothesis Table where the Holy Gifts were prepared, and where, until this point, the Gifts have remained covered with veils. During the censing and this movement to the Prothesis, the people have been singing the Cherubic Hymn: a sublime hymn that prepares us for entry into the holiest of mysteries as representatives of the Cherubim (one of the orders of angels in the heavenly host), which concludes when priest, deacon, and servers have made their procession with the Gifts and are standing before the Holy Doors. Once here, as those who processed stand in place, the commemorations are made, whereby the list of those being prayed for at that Liturgy is read out. Importantly, this list always includes the name of the bishop under whose oversight the community falls (be it a parish, a mission, or a monastery), as commemorating him is to signify communion with him, and without an Orthodox bishop, there is no Orthodox community.[21] Finally, once the commemorations have concluded, the procession returns to the Altar – the priest and deacon through the Holy Doors; the servers through the other doors – the Gifts are placed on the Holy Table and censed, the Doors are

---

[21] In dioceses of the Russian tradition, it is most common to include a commemoration of the Patriarch followed by the local Metropolitan, together with the diocesan (local) bishop, in hierarchical order. This is distinct from Greek practice, where only the diocesan bishop tends to be commemorated at a parish Liturgy.

closed and the curtain drawn, and the Liturgy continues.

With the Holy Gifts now set out and censed, the Litany of Supplication is offered by the deacon, beginning with the words, 'For the precious gifts here set forth, let us pray to the Lord', after which the curtain is drawn back. There is then an invitation to confess the Faith of the Church in the words of the Nicene Creed, which leads into the Anaphora.

The Anaphora is the climactic moment of the Divine Liturgy, and a prayer without parallel. Indeed, if we were to go looking for a summary of Orthodox Christian belief in terms of what the Creed looks like in action, we would need to look no further than the Anaphora. Although I have never found the source, I have heard it said that the early Irish Christians called the Anaphora, 'the most dangerous prayer'; and whether or not this is true, it is entirely reasonable. For in the Anaphora, the Church prays directly to God the Father. In the Anaphora, we ask for God to make himself directly and truly known among us in the common elements of bread and wine. In the Anaphora, we encounter the actions of all three Persons of the Holy Trinity. It is a supreme act of faith. There really is nothing to which it can be compared.

In the Orthodox Church, there are two anaphorae used most often: that of St John Chrysostom, which we use almost every week, and that of St Basil the Great, which we use on ten occasions throughout the year. The second of these is significantly longer, and is arguably the most thorough embodiment of the Orthodox Faith to be found in a single prayer. The first, however, although shorter and consequently less thorough, is no less abundant in spiritual fruit. At the same time, both follow the same structure.

Regardless of whether we use the Anaphora of St John Chrysostom or St Basil, it follows the same pattern:

1. Dialogue between priest and people, beginning with 'The grace of our Lord Jesus Christ, and the love of God, and the communion of the Holy Spirit be with all of you', and continuing with the invitation to, '…lift up our hearts'

2. The preface, in which God is praised, a brief account of His saving acts is recited, and a tone of thanksgiving is set

3. The people respond to this with the song of the angels, commonly called the 'Sanctus', which runs, 'Holy, holy, holy Lord of Sabaoth: heaven and earth are full of Thy glory…'

4. The 'institution narrative' is recited by the priest, which begins with a brief account of God in Jesus Christ, leading into the words Jesus Himself offered at the Last Supper. In response to these, the people respond with, 'Amen'

5. The 'anamnesis', or act of remembrance, is proclaimed, in which we recall that we do what we are doing in memory of the Lord's own acts, concluding with the raising of the Gifts in offering

6. Central to the Anaphora, then, is the epiclesis, at which point the priest asks that the Holy Spirit might be sent down upon the

Gifts, thereby changing them into the Body and Blood of Jesus Christ[22]

7. Now, in the presence of the Lord on the Holy Table, are offered the intercessions, beginning with the saints together with the Irmos (a hymn to the Theotokos), and including the whole Church and all the living and the dead

8. The Anaphora concludes with the Doxology – the proclamation of God in Three Persons – to which all the people say 'Amen'.

Once this extraordinary prayer has come to an end, there is another Litany of Supplication followed by the Lord's Prayer, then some final preparations made by the priest in advance of receiving Communion. These final preparations are undertaken behind the curtain, before it and the Holy Doors are opened and left that way until the end of the Liturgy. For by the presence of the Lord,

---

[22] In Russian practice, the Epiclesis is preceded by a recitation of the prayer of the Third Hour, in which the priest says, 'O Lord, who at the third hour didst send down Thy most Holy Spirit upon Thine Apostles…'. In Greek practice, the priest moves directly from the elevation of the Gifts into the Epiclesis.

the separation between heaven and earth is undone, and we partake fully in the life of heaven by means of His own Body and Blood.

There are, of course, many other services offered by the Orthodox Church. These might include matins, vespers, and compline (the Hours), an akathist (a service featuring a hymn for a particular saint or event in the Church's life), a moleben (a service of prayer for a particular intention), a panikhyda (a service for the dead),[23] and others. All of these services, however, might be thought of as liturgies with a lower case 'L', in contrast with the Divine Liturgy, which we should always think of in upper case. Ultimately, while the liturgical life of the Orthodox Church is rich and varied, and while its many facets address all sorts and conditions of men, the Divine Liturgy is the summit of its life, and the supreme mystery by which we encounter heavenly reality on earth.

---

[23] All of these services will have different names in different traditions. A moleben, for example, which is from Slavonic, is called in Greek a 'paraklesis'.

10.

Monasticism

It has been said by more than one person that, 'the Church is only as healthy as its monasteries'. There are many reasons for this, but one of the main ones is that Orthodox monastics stand as a testament to the power of the Christian life well lived. And this is something that pertains to all Orthodox, regardless of each person's specific vocation. In fact, in his book, *Orthodoxy*, Paul Evdokimov declares that all Orthodox Christians are called to lead a monastic life. He is not the first, nor the only, person to say so, but his magisterial work on the tradition of the Church certainly makes it particularly striking as an idea. But what does he mean by it?

Considering the popular notion that monasticism equals, simply, celibacy, it is important to make clear that it is not this to which Evdokimov is referring. Indeed, George Florovsky, in *The Ascetic Ideal and the New Testament*, reminds us that

> *Celibacy is a part of the monastic life and it too has its source in the teachings of the New Testament. In I Corinthians 7: 1-11 St. Paul encourages both marriage and celibacy—both are forms of Christian spirituality, and St. Paul has much to say about marriage in his other epistles. But his point is that celibacy is a form of spirituality for some, and it therefore cannot be excluded from the forms of spirituality within the Church…. The monastic practice of celibacy is precisely not excluded by the New Testament. Rather, it is even encouraged both by our Lord and by St Paul—and without jeopardy to the married state. The decision cannot be forced. Rather, it must come from the heart. And, indeed, it is not for everyone.*

In concert with this, Evdokimov is saying that the monastic way of asceticism and prayer, of humility and virtue, of self-restraint and liturgical participation, is fundamental to the Orthodox life, whether a person is a monk, a nun, a priest, deacon, or lay person. It could be said, then, that monasticism in Orthodoxy is about these latter things above all. But it is also about much more than that.

The monastic ideal is an ancient one. It can be found, first of all, in the example of the Old Testament prophets, who dedicated themselves to attentiveness to God's revelation, and were often to be found at the periphery of the wider community. It is this life of communion with God and observation of the community from which the prophets drew their power. As regarding its translation into a Christian context Florovsky says in the same essay, 'The life of the early Church as described in the Acts of the Apostles is so clear that no analysis or presentation of texts is necessary to demonstrate that the essentials exist for a form of spirituality similar to that of monastic and ascetical Christianity'. The Christian monk, from the very beginning, did as the prophets did and kept to this early Christian ideal by explicitly pursuing progression through spiritual purification to illumination to deification by means of constant prayer, participation in the sacraments, and obedience.

Even as we enumerate these monastic activities, however, the contemporary world is such that they will be almost incomprehensible to most people. Western society, after all, hardly facilitates an understanding of the inner life, inclined as it is to constant material stimulation. We are surrounded by technology with all of its corresponding temptations; we can hardly escape the sexual imagery and discourse displayed on our screens and bus stop posters; whether we want to or not, we are forced to navigate the demands of everything from mortgages to car finance to our resource consumption. Yet in the midst of this, the call to follow Christ and be perfect beckons. And when we are unable to respond, the monk does for us.

This in no way excuses Orthodox Christians from working to conform their lives to that of Christ; it does not mean that, in any sense, we are absolved from the challenges of living well. It means something more akin to the words of St Ephraim of

Katounakia, an elder of Mount Athos who knew well the rigours of a life of asceticism. 'If I read a hundred prayers in the silence of Athos a day, and you, in the noise of the city, with work and family responsibilities, read three prayers, then we are in the same position.' That is to say, Orthodox people living in the world strive for the same purpose and to the same end as monastics, but according to their capacity while taking account of the necessities of life. The monk or nun, by contrast, living in the context of a monastery, is able to focus without distraction on the three states to which all are called: purification and illumination, leading to deification. In the process, they are also able to pray not only for themselves and the concerns most close to them, but for the whole world.

An interesting facet of Orthodox monasticism is that there are no 'orders' as there are in the Catholic West. There are no Benedictines, Carmelites, Franciscans, or Dominicans, for example. An Orthodox monk or nun may pursue one of three traditional monastic paths: anchoritic (the solitary life), cenobitic (communal life), or in a skete (a combination of the anchoritic and cenobitic, where monastics live alone, but worship together).

The degrees of monasticism, meanwhile, generally reflect the level of experience he or she has attained in the spiritual life, and begin with the novitiate. A *novice* is clothed in a simple cassock and skufia (soft, brimless hat), and sometimes a leather belt. A prayer rope is also given, to be used for the recitation of the Jesus Prayer. The rite of tonsuring takes place and a new, monastic, name is given when the novice becomes a *rassophore*, which means that he or she is now expected to enter permanently into the monastic life. At this point, the clothing also changes to that which we normally associate with Orthodox monastics: the outer cassock with wide, flowing sleeves, and the klobuk, a stiff, brimless hat covered with a long veil that hangs down the back. The leather belt is also a feature of this habit. Vows are normally only made when the rassophore becomes a *stavrophore*, at which point a wooden hand Cross and beeswax candle are also given. The final stage of monastic life is called the *Great Schema*, which only comes about when it is judged that the monk or nun has attained the necessary level of maturity in spiritual matters. It includes the wearing of an 'analavos', which is a long cloth that hangs down the front and back of the habit, over the shoulders of the wearer. This cloth bears the embroidered symbols of the Passion of Christ, as well as the words of the Trisagion. Importantly, men and women are vested in the same habit as each other across all degrees. From the time a monk enters the novitiate, meanwhile, he tends to be called 'Father', whether or not he is a priest, while nuns from the rank of stavrophore are called 'Mother'. When a monk is also a priest or deacon, he is called a hieromonk or hierodeacon. Bishops of the Orthodox Church are normally drawn from the ranks of monastic clergy.

Ultimately, monasticism serves the Church by modelling the Orthodox Christian life, by doing the things that those who live their life in the world cannot always do, and by praying for the world as it goes about its daily business. In the midst of this, individual monastics might share the spiritual gifts that have been bestowed on them through their dedication to holy things by acting as spiritual fathers and mothers to the spiritual inquirers who come to them. Remember: this does not absolve Orthodox Christians from doing what they need to do themselves, but it does mean that when they are unable, the spiritual work is still being done. In this respect, there is a symbiotic relationship between monasticism and the life of the Church in the world that draws us back to the idea with which this chapter began: that 'the Church is only as healthy as its monasteries.'

11.

Icons

In the first chapter of this book, icons were described as being one of the single most distinctive features of Orthodox worship. When you were invited to imagine walking into an Orthodox temple for the first time, it was said that one of the first things you would notice when looking toward the front (or East end) of the building is the iconostasis: that screen or wall that separates the nave from the Altar. It was also said that you would likely see icons all around you: on walls, on stands, and even on embroidered banners. Indeed, if you were there with a practicing Orthodox Christian, you would likely see the icons being venerated – that is, this Orthodox person might cross themselves and bow, before kissing an icon.

Why, though? What is it about these images that sees them afforded such importance in Orthodox life and worship?

The first thing to be said about icons is that, when the faithful bow before them and kiss them, they are in no way worshipping them. Any accusation that the Orthodox worship wood and paint needs to be laid to rest. It is true that we treat them as sacred, but what we do with them is veneration; NOT worship. The Church has actually been clear about this from the beginning. Worship is reserved for God alone (called in Latin, *latria*), while veneration is what we offer saints, angels, and the faithful servants of God (called in Latin, *dulia*). And when we stand before an icon, because what we see is an image of the Incarnate Lord or one of His servants, we are paying our respects; communicating the regard in which we hold them.

Icons are often called 'windows into heaven', and while this is an apt description, it should be considered with all the corresponding implications.

This is because icons do not enable *direct* access to the person being venerated, but *in*direct – reflecting the separation that exists between this world and the next. The communion with the holy ones the icons enable, however, is akin to seeing someone through glass: it allows us to interact with them in love whilst still acknowledging the reality that we are separated by the veil between this life and the afterlife. For as members of the Body of Christ, the whole Church – visible and invisible – we are spiritually united regardless of physical separation. The kiss we place on an icon, therefore, is a kiss transmitted to the person depicted. An analogy might be with an old photo of a loved one. The widower who reminisces about his late wife might find a photo album and out of love for her, kiss the picture taken of her on a fondly-remembered holiday. In this case, he is not confusing the photograph with the person, but moved by love, is wishing she was there with him and expressing that love in the only way he can at the time. The difference between the widower's situation, and that of the Orthodox Christian venerating an icon, though, is in the mystical communion we share with them in Christ. When the

Orthodox person, moved by love, venerates the icon of a saint, that love is truly shared and experienced.

That this is so is attested to by the fact that in earliest Christian worship, walls were adorned with the images of Christ and His saints, as well as scenes from the Holy Scriptures. The catacombs in Rome and the house church in Dura-Europas (dating from the early third century), for example, contain images of Christ, scenes from the Gospels, and the prophets of the Old Testament. Such images denoted real communion with the people and events depicted. This use of imagery, meanwhile, has a deep lineage in the Jewish tradition out of which Christianity grew. The synagogue in Dura-Europas, dating from the same period as the house church there (making it one of the oldest in the world), is adorned with images, while we can look as far back as Exodus and the construction of the Ark of the Covenant to see that the ritual use of physical things – images, materials, and symbols – were not just deployed, but were even commanded by God. Finally, by the time of the seventh Ecumenical Council, held at Nicaea in A.D. 787, icons are declared by the Church to be something fundamental to the life of the Church.

The question is: why? Why do icons come to be not just an aesthetic 'extra' sometimes used by the Church, but something so important they are ultimately recognised as essential?

The answer to this lies in the Incarnation. When the Second Person of the Trinity took on matter, He re-consecrated matter as a worthy medium for His representation. Matter – the *stuff* of creation – was united with the divine life by means of the Nativity, Crucifixion, Resurrection, and Ascension, and the reciprocity inherent in this act entails that we are able to apprehend the divine life in matter. Of course, this same reciprocity can be traced all the way back to creation, and especially when humanity is established in His image and likeness, and when creation is declared to be 'good'. The first disobedience – commonly called 'the Fall' – of course, undermines this reciprocal relationship, but it is reestablished in the Incarnation. Our use of icons, then, becomes an expression of our faith in the Incarnation. For this reason, the last of the ecumenical councils which, amongst other things, established how we should understand the Incarnation, declared the use of icons to be *de fide* – of the essence of the Faith.

At the same time, the idea of the icon plays an even bigger role in Orthodox theology, as Orthodox Christians read the world iconologically. The lens through which we interpret the nature of the world and the Church is much the same as that through which we experience the paintings of saints, angels, and Christ Himself when we encounter them in the Temple or in our homes.

If matter – that is, the 'stuff' of creation – has been united to divinity in the Incarnation, then in matter we can see the image of God. From the smallest particle to the greatest star, from the smallest cell to the greatest living creature, the image of God can be found within. Staring with the expanse of the universe, then narrowing it down to solid matter, then from solid matter to living matter, then to animals and on to humans, to the constituted Church – that is, those who have responded to the call to embody the icon of Christ as members of His Body – to the ordained ministers of the Church who serve to make manifest His real presence in the midst of the world, and ultimately to the bishops whose role is to manifest the whole ministry of the Church in their person, everything we see and experience is drawn into an iconological economy, varying in its participation in God's work in the Incarnation only by degree. The following six diagrams illustrate what this might look like:

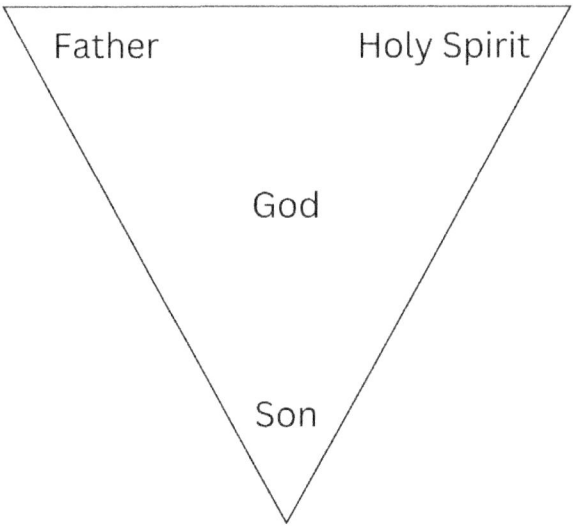

fig. 1 God is.

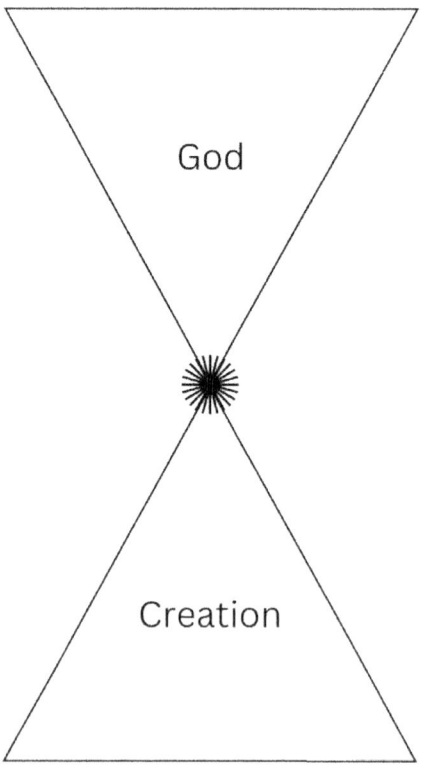

fig. 2: God establishes creation in His image, and declares it to be good.

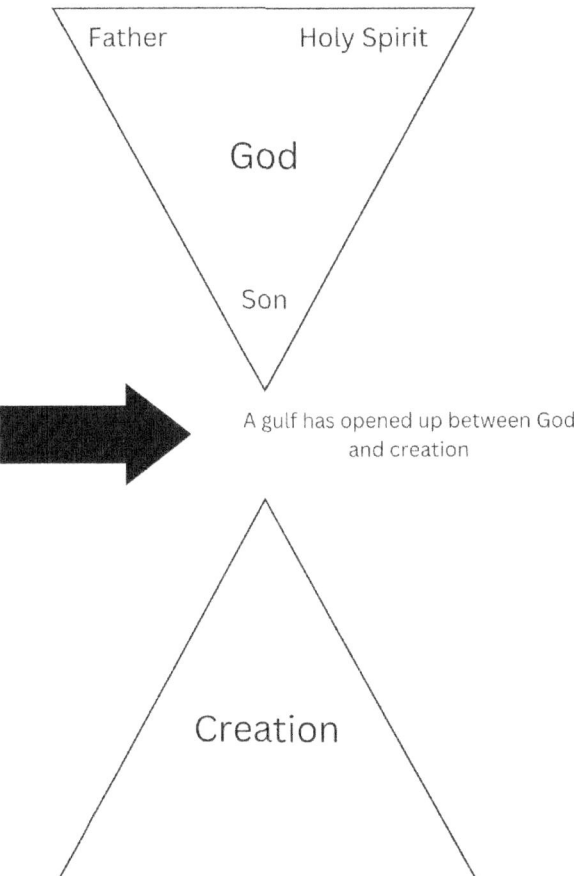

fig. 3: Humanity falls and brings down creation so that it is no longer in God's full image.

Father   Holy Spirit

God

Son

A gulf has opened up between God and creation

Creation

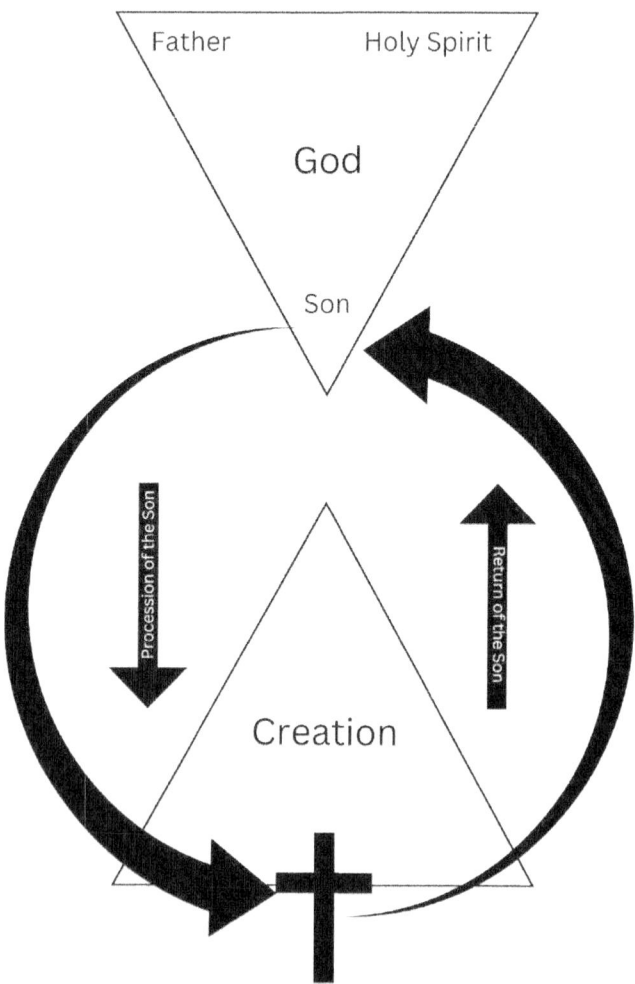

fig. 4: God sends His Son into the world (creation) to reconcile us to God by taking on creation itself

Father　　　　Holy Spirit

God

Son

Procession of the Son

Return of the Son

Creation

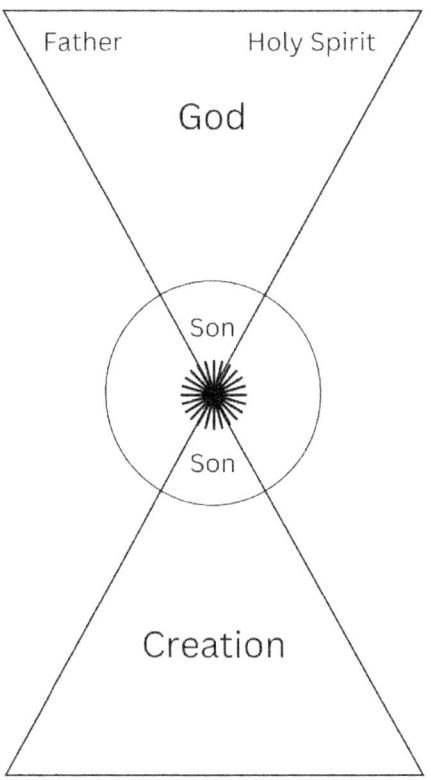

fig. 5: The Son becomes the meeting point between God and creation / Divinity and humanity

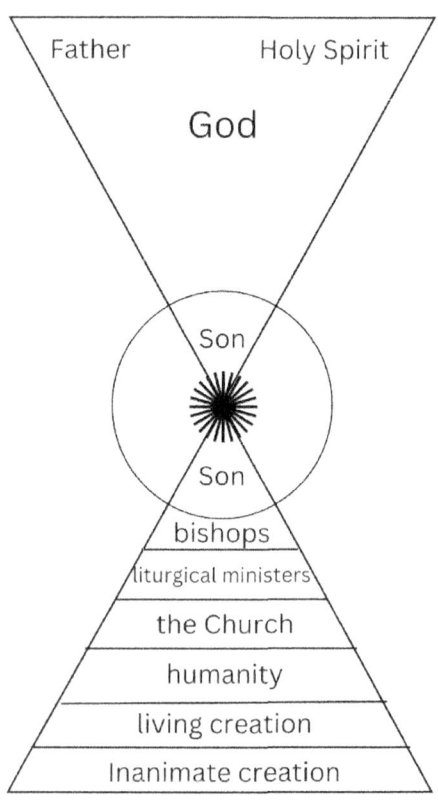

fig. 6: The image of God in creation now restored, it is possible to see more clearly how creation reflects God.

What we have, then, is a cosmological order in which God can be seen – a role taken up in a *particular* way by the Church.

So, Orthodoxy sees the world iconologically – that is, it perceives and even communes with God in all that God has made. According to this view of the world, every person is a living icon of God, most especially because each person bears the same nature that God chose to take on for Himself. At the same time, the Orthodox designate specific types of images to serves as icons in the context of worship, whether that worship takes place in the temple, the home, a car, or the office. We do this because, as we can see in the diagram immediately above, the more particular the form of matter, the more specific the use. While God can be perceived in subatomic particles, those particles are both out of reach of most people's perception, and even when they can be apprehended, require an application of the intellect equally out of reach. It becomes easier when we move into more recognisable forms of matter, and easiest of all when it comes to human beings.

When human beings participate in God's creative process, by painting icons for example, then they become even more apparent in their iconological role. That which they produce, meanwhile – especially when set aside by holy intention – follows suit. This means that something like a painting of Jesus, the angels, or the saints, dedicated by means of its style and purpose, serves in the very particular function of an icon such as we use in worship. In this respect, the icon is like (though not exactly like) a sacrament, which also takes material things and sees them effectively set aside (by means of certain prayers) as conveyers of divine reality. In the constant, reciprocal flow of imagination, then, the image of God can be apprehended in all things, while liturgical icons serve as a locus for this apprehension.

It is for this reason that icons need to be understood, not only as tools within worship as objects for veneration, but as representative of the entire Orthodox worldview.

Conclusion

The Orthodox Church is the second-largest single body of Christians in the world, with over two hundred million adherents. Made up of a number of national Churches, it not only claims to maintain the ancient traditions of the Church, but *to be* the living Church as it was called out of the world by Christ and proliferated by St Paul and the holy apostles. It inherits that which was revealed first to the ancient Hebrews, by accepting the law and the prophets, yet understanding their fulfilment in the Incarnation. It was the Orthodox Church that established the Holy Scriptures as we know them, and the Orthodox

Church that elucidated the doctrines of God that Christians subscribe to today. Ultimately, the Orthodox Church is not a denomination of Christianity, but Christianity itself as it was established from the beginning.

This will likely sound to many readers like an arrogant claim. Yet to make it is simply to attest to history. The bishops and theologians who attended the councils were indeed none other than those of the undivided Church. The doctrines fundamental to Christianity today were defined at those councils. And which body of Christians can say that they continue to hold them unchanged since except the Orthodox? Who can say that their celebration of the Eucharist evolved directly out of the practices of the Jewish Temple and synagogue but the Orthodox, as they serve the Divine Liturgy? Whose beliefs and practices have remained unchanged since they emerged from the ancient places of the Eastern Mediterranean in the first centuries of Church life? The Orthodox.

For all that, it is not as if the Orthodox Church does not have its troubles and challenges. The late nineteenth century witnessed the designation of a new heresy – namely 'ethnophyletism' – whereby ethnicity is considered ahead of the doctrine of the Church, and it remains an issue today. The fact that in the Western world, where Orthodoxy has expanded over the last number of centuries, there are dioceses and jurisdictions based on countries of origin as opposed to the land in which the Church finds itself today is a testament to this. Then, the fact that a Pan-Orthodox council, held in Crete in 2016, failed to get the support of the Moscow Patriarchate, as well as the Churches of Antioch, Bulgaria, Georgia, together with the current rift between the patriarchate of Moscow and Constantinople, underscores the tensions that persist among the Orthodox.

Most important, though, is precisely the fact that none of these situations bears directly on the content of the Gospel being announced and the Christian life being lived on the ground in Orthodox communities. The deposit of faith continues to be believed and proclaimed and the Divine Liturgy continues to be served as they have been since the apostles first emerged from Jerusalem and evolved in the centuries thereafter. Since the Faith spread around the Mediterranean world, the Nicene Creed was promulgated and further councils articulated the right understanding of God and the Person and Work of Christ, and the forms of service developed, nothing has changed. The Orthodox Church has challenges to overcome, but through it all it maintains, and has always maintained, the same Faith and practice.

Hopefully, this book has given you a sense for why the Orthodox Church is worth getting to know. We started by using our imaginations as we sought to orient ourselves within an Orthodox space. At that time, possibly everything was new and strange; now, armed with some awareness of what the Church thinks, what the Church does, and why, experiencing it should not feel nearly so daunting. Yet, even having made it through these pages, real knowledge of the Church only comes through living its life. Religion is never just a thing to be read about if one really wants to know it; it is a living thing that must be experienced, and this is arguably true of Orthodoxy more than any other form of Christianity. For Orthodoxy, as we have seen, is not comprised of a series of propositions to which we can simply assent. Rather, it is a life of prayer and worship, thought and action, that shapes our very being.

St Paul said concerning knowledge of God, '…now we see in a mirror, dimly, but then face to face' (1 Corinthians 13:12). Like any book on the subject, this one has been a mirror. It is to our benefit to go deeper, so that we might come to know Orthodoxy face to face.

.

Suggestions for Further Reading

The following suggestions represent just a few works that will allow you to explore more fully the ideas that have been presented to you in this book. Aside from Metropolitan Kallistos' two books, together with Schmemann's 'For the Life of the World', the others here might be considered 'academic'. They are not, however, impossible to understand, and can be infinitely fruitful to those who try them. If you are in doubt as to whether or not they are right for you, perhaps ask a local priest if you can borrow them, or pay a visit to the library.

General

The Orthodox Church, by Kallistos Ware

The Orthodox Way, by Kallistos Ware

The Orthodox Church, by John McGuckin

Orthodoxy, by Paul Evdokimov

Theology

Introducing Eastern Orthodox Theology, by Andrew Louth

Deification in Christ, by Panayiotis Nellas

The Deification of Man, by Georgios Mantzaridis

Liturgy

For the Light of the World, by Alexander Schmemann

The Orthodox Liturgy, by Hugh Wybrew

The Euchologion Unveiled, by Job Getcha

Icons

The Art of the Icon, by Paul Evdokimov

Gazing on God, by Andreas Andreopoulos

Iconostasis, by Pavel Florensky

Christ and the Councils

Christ in Eastern Christian Thought, by John Meyendorff

The Mystery of Christ, by John Behr

The Bible

The Whole Counsel of God, by Stephen de Young

The Message of the Bible, by George Cronk

Printed in Great Britain
by Amazon

46672952R00078